M000238083

The Honest Bengal Cat Guide For Humans

Bengal Cat and Kitten Care

Written by Shirley O'Connor
The Bengal Cat

Copyright Information

Published by ROC Publishing 2017

Copyright and Trademarks

This publication is **Copyright 2017** by **ROC Publishing**. All products, publications, software and services mentioned and recommended in this publication are protected by trademarks. In such instance, all trademarks & copyright belong to the respective owners.
All rights reserved. No part of this book may be reproduced or transferred in any form or by any means, graphic, electronic, or mechanical including photocopying, recording, taping, or by any information storage retrieval system, without the written permission of the author. Pictures used in this book are either royalty free pictures bought from stock-photo websites or have the source mentioned underneath the picture.

Disclaimer and Legal Notice

This product is not legal or medical advice and should not be interpreted in that manner. You need to do your own due-diligence to determine if the content of this product is right for you. The author and the affiliates of this product are not liable for any damages or losses associated with the content of this product. While every attempt has been made to verify the information shared in this publication, neither the author nor the affiliates assume any responsibility for errors, omissions or contrary interpretation of the subject matter herein. Any perceived slights to any specific person(s) or organization(s) are purely unintentional. We have no control over the nature, content and availability of the web sites listed in this book. The inclusion of any website links does not necessarily imply a recommendation or endorse the views expressed within them. ROC Publishing takes no responsibility for, and will not be liable for, the websites being temporarily unavailable or being removed from the Internet.
The accuracy and completeness of information provided herein are not guaranteed or warranted to produce any particular results, and the advice and strategies, contained herein may not be suitable for every individual. The author shall not be liable for any loss incurred as a consequence of the use and application, directly or indirectly, of any information presented in this work. The publication is designed to provide information in regards to the subject matter covered.

Acknowledgments

Thank you to my most favourite and loyal humans – Sue and Zoe, you have been my inspiration and energy; particularly and very importantly a fantastic provider of food, cuddles and fun. Also to Jo and Andrew, literally the best next-door neighbours EVER, not only did you give a home to Heidi (sorry couldn't stand her any longer) but you come and play with me when I'm all alone.

Good luck and congratulations all BENGAL CAT owners around the world, you lucky humans – I hope this book comes in useful....

Table of Contents

Foreword from Shirley

When a human hears the word "Bengal," they immediately think of TIGERS and JUNGLES. Admit it, you do.

That's because the Bengal cat is such an exceptional breed; we are instantly recognisable by our beautiful markings, playful personality, and affinity for water (you've guessed it, just like the TIGER). Actually, you should be thinking more Asian Leopard Cat if I'm honest, but easy mistake.

Bengals are relatively new on our planet, especially in the world of registered cat breeds, we were actually only recognised as a breed in the 1970s.

We're still Bengal babies...

I am a proud guardian of a Human Being named Susan O'Connor, Susan is my mum and has decided to call me Shirley O'Connor. Well, at least that's what she thinks, let me tell you, I'm a little embarrassed and it's not what my other feline friends know me as, I'd be the laughing stock of the street if that was the case.

Although Susan and her other human companions have brought me incredible joy over the years I sometimes feel they just don't get me and could do with a bit more education in the world of the Bengal. I always hear her friends asking WHY I'm doing something, so I thought it'd be much easier if I just sat down and wrote a guide book for you all.

I'm very attached to my humans, as well as my best friend, Pepsi the Standard Poodle and I wanted to share with you the joys of having a Bengal cat (especially one like me).

I wish you all luck and excitement in your Bengal adventures, you will NEVER BE SORRY.

CHAPTER ONE: History

The History of Bengal Cats

Hi there! I'm Shirley, and as I have a lot of first-hand knowledge on Bengal cats – I am one, after all – so, I'm going to take a second to explain our history to you. After all, sometimes the best way to get to know someone is by learning where they come from, right?

To start off with, let's take a look at the bigger Bengal picture... So, where do Bengal cats actually come from?

The name makes you think of something WILD, doesn't it? Something exotic and untameable! Something magnificent and gorgeous! Something like...well, ME actually.

Let's start with a timeline and keep this simple.

Back in the late 1800s, some people started cross breeding Asian leopard cats with domestic cats. They would then backcross, and backcross the cats again to create what would later be known as the Bengal cat.

What does BACKCROSSING mean?

I'm glad I did some research, because I have to be honest, as clever as I am, I wasn't so sure what it meant, either.

Backcrossing is when a hybrid is crossbred with one of its parents or with another cat that is genetically similar to its parents. That's done twice to create the Bengal cat breed.

In 1889, and author named Harrison Weir talked about Bengal cats in his book "Our Cats and All About Them". It's worth talking about our ancestors, too. The Asian leopard cats.

Prionailurus bengalensis is the fancy schmancy scientific name for the Asian leopard cat. What a mouthful. These cats find their home in South and East Asia and are well and truly WILD. Leopard cats have longer legs than I do and they're a little more slender. What's a girl to do, though, when she's got it made in the shade and doesn't have to hunt for a living?

These cats' ears have little rounded tips like some domestic cat breeds. They're also known for their markings which can vary from subspecies to subspecies of leopard cat.

They are about the same size as a domestic cat in terms of height and length, which would make it awfully easy for someone to confuse me for one of these wilder things.

The Asian leopard cats make their homes in just about every habitat. They can be found in the mountains of Nepal and the foothills of other Asian countries. They like forests, rivers, and even some snow, but if the snow is more than 10 centimetres in height, they will avoid that area and I don't blame them either.

There was one study done where Asian leopard cats were caught on camera at over 10,000 feet in altitude! That's crazy! The highest I've ever been is about 8 feet up in the air when I climbed our garden tree and yes, I fell; although being true to my nature I landed on all fours of course...

Asian leopard cats are known for being solitary. They like to hunt alone and they usually do it at night. Their favourite things to catch are tree shrews, rabbits, small mammals, lizards, and other small prey. YUM. They are carnivorous.

They're known for liking to climb trees and have been found catching prey up to 10 feet up in a tree. I'm not surprised at all considering that some of them aren't even scared of mountains!

Over 5,000 years ago in China, the first cat was domesticated and it happens to have been an Asian leopard cat. The history of my breed goes back way beyond the writings of Harrison Weird, apparently, we made great companions then and we make great companions now, too.

Asian Leopard Cat

OK, so, let's jump forward quite a bit in time to the 1970s...

Feline leukaemia is a big concern for anyone with a cat and all cats should get vaccinated for it. In the 1970s, a scientist named William Centerwall was breeding Asian leopard cats with domestic cats because they seemed to have an immunity to feline leukaemia, or at least they didn't catch it as easily.

A man named Bill Engler took note of this and also wanted to preserve the rare genetics of the Asian leopard cat. This man chose the name "Bengal" for the breed of cats that he created. These aren't the same Bengals that are recognized as a breed today, but they are an important piece of the history of the Bengal cat.

There were two other breeders, Greg and Elizabeth Kent who bred the Asian leopard cat with the Egyptian Mau. An Egyptian Mau called "Heidi-Pi" is actually my next-door neighbour, honest. These cats went on to be a special kind of Bengal cat and have descendants still here today, i.e. the beautiful moi....

The International Cat Association recognized the Bengal breed officially in 1983. Jean Mill played a large role in this. She wanted to take the hybrid cats and actually domesticate them instead of just breeding wild cats with domesticated ones.

One interesting thing to note, that I think is complete hogwash, is that the Cat Fanciers' Association won't recognize the Bengal because we have an obvious wild ancestor!

There are 60,000 registered Bengals in the world today and they are an incredibly popular breed. Why wouldn't we be, after all? Soon, I'm going to tell you just what makes us so special.

The History of Me

Here's a bit about my history. I did promise after all...

To cut a long story short, I was rescued by my humans from a cat sanctuary when I was just eight months old. I was in a cage, all alone before I spotted them. They spotted my spots and fell in love.... who wouldn't?

Right away I knew they were the ones for me. I was a shy little thing, but I tried my best to be brave and curious. I didn't even know what a hand was at first, it took me three weeks to come out from behind the cupboard when they collected me.

Remember, I came from a very insecure background, where I received no love or affection. I don't remember much about those times as I have so many happy memories to replace them now. I can talk about it a little now that I have a secure base here in Manchester.

I was so shy that at first, my humans thought I didn't speak. But then once I started I just couldn't stop. In fact, when they first started giving me food, I was so excited that I screamed the house down and jumped all over them, it must have been the joy of my wild side coming out. (Did I mention I'm also very clever, I love to have a read of the paper on a Sunday).

CHAPTER TWO: Appearance

One of the first things that people tell my human Susan, when they meet me is what a completely good-looking girl I am. I'd rather be called handsome if I'm honest, but never mind, it's just semantics after all. I really do try and not to let it get to my head, but I'll just say I have seen myself in a mirror and they honestly aren't lying.

We Bengal cats are known for our distinctive colourings and markings. There are several varieties of looks that you can find on a Bengal cat! For one breed, we are very diverse.

Size & Weight

While you should never ask a cat how much she weighs, Bengals are a bit larger than the average domestic cat.

Male Bengals can weigh 10–15 lbs (4.5–6.8kg), and females like myself can weigh anywhere between 8–12 lbs (3.6–5.4 kg). Sometimes we might be bigger or smaller than this, so you shouldn't worry if your Bengal isn't between these guidelines!

We are strong, athletic cats, and should be fairly slender in build. Our back legs are a little longer than our front ones, so our backs arch a little when standing in given positions.

Our heads are pretty small in comparison to our bodies, and our ears are small too – that's thanks to our ancestors!

Markings

Something distinctive about Bengals is our stripes. Some stripes are horizontal (typical of marbled Bengals) and some spots are sort of like a leopard's. Remember how we're related to the Asian leopard cat? Well, that's where we get these kinds of markings!

There are a couple of important things to note about the markings that we Bengals can have. Something that we all have is the M-marking on our foreheads.

This is just two markings above each of our eyes that form the shape of an M. The markings are typically the darkest shade of markings on our bodies. It can be subtle, but at the same time, once you know what to look for, you'll see it on every Bengal you meet.

You can see it really clearly on my cousin, Clarence. Such a show off.

One thing that Bengals have in common is that our stomach is white. Don't be afraid to give us a belly rub, (although I have to admit I really don't like it) just note that too much can get you a snappy bite or two – but don't worry, we're just playing (most of the time). More on that later.

Something else important to know about our markings is that we all wear mascara.

Just kidding. Not real mascara, anyway. We have a marking around our eyes that is referred to as mascara. This is referring to the horizontal stripes that are beside our eyes.

Colour

There are three colours that are "recognised" Bengal colours, but there are also some colours that can show up from time to time through recessive genes that are considered "unrecognised". The recognised colours are brown, silver and snow…

Brown Bengals with brown fur will most likely have green or golden eyes, and they usually have a black or dark brown spotted or marble pattern.

Silver Bengals with silver fur will have an almost white, silver or silvery background colour with an inky black spotted or marble pattern. Silver Bengals will also have green or golden eyes.

Snow Bengals with snow fur can have one of three distinct genetic variations…

Seal lynx point is the lightest of the group. Kittens with this genetic makeup will be born with white fur or very faint markings as their pattern comes in later. As they get older, seal lynx point Bengals will have brownish-grey or tan spotted/marble patterns on a white or cream background. They're also the only Bengal variation to have ice blue eyes.

Seal mink Bengals are normally born with a distinctive pattern that gets darker as they age. They are usually an ivory or cream colour with caramel-chocolate patterns. Seal mink Bengals have aqua or green eyes.

Seal sepia is the darkest of the three variations, and these Bengals are often born with a distinct seal brown/dark brown pattern. These Bengals have golden or green eyes.

There are also some really beautiful "non-recognised" colours...

Charcoal Bengals strike up debate amongst some people. While it is believed by some to be the result of a separate genetic colour, others attribute it as the darkest range on the spectrum of recognised colours, i.e. 'charcoal brown' or 'charcoal silver'. Charcoal Bengals will have very dark grey/brown fur and have dark masks. With spotted Charcoals, you can often see they have a dark stripe going down their back called a cape!

Melanistic / black Bengals with this colour will have black backgrounds and very faint brown-black patterns which are often hard to see unless under natural light.

Blue Bengals are described as having a "buttery-peachy" background and light bluish-grey markings that never turn black. Because this colour never appears in wild cats, it is discounted as a "recognised" colour in domestics.

Bengal patterns

There are four colours of Bengals:

Snow marble, silver rosettes, blue rosettes, and brown rosettes.

Whew! That seems like a lot! How can you tell the difference?

To be marbled means that you have the markings typical of a normal tabby cat, but they are swirled. They look sort of like an impressionist painting!

Like if Vincent Van Gogh painted a really beautiful cat.

Snow marble

I have a friend name Mia who is a snow marble. She's absolutely stunning, if I do say so myself. Her human mum is very proud of her. We haven't met in person (or should I say "in cat") yet, we just communicate on the internet, but I would seriously love to get to play with her someday. Last night I dreamt we were dancing together under the light of the cheesy moon.

She's got a white base to her coat, or perhaps an off white. Her spots and swirls are light tan all the way to a dark, almost black, brown. The markings extend all the way from her forehead to her hindquarters. Her tail is dark brown on top and on the bottom, it's white like her stomach. Just like all Bengal cats.

Mia really likes her picture to be taken. She poses like a wild cat. Like an Asian leopard cat. The only difference is that when she poses, it's indoors and not outside in the jungle, though I'm pretty sure all of us Bengal cats would be just as comfortable running around the jungle as we are in our homes and backyards. We're very curious.

I have another friend who is Mia's brother. His name is Phoenix. He's also a snow marble. Phoenix almost looks like he could be a snow leopard. His markings are much lighter than Mia's. They range from off white all the way to dark tan and he has swirling patterns that run all the way down his body. Even though he and his sister are very different, they're both beautiful, just like me.

Types of marble pattern

Tri-colour & quad-colour patterns indicate that there are three or four definite colours on the Bengal's coat; the background, the marble markings and the centre of those markings.

Horizontal flowing is where the marble pattern flows down horizontally from the upper shoulder along the body to the back of the cat.

High acreage / reduced pattern is where there is a lot of background pattern showing behind and between the marble pattern. This is seen as being the most similar to our wild ancestors and so is highly desirable.

Chaos patterns are made up of swirls and splashes in a whole bunch of different sizes and shapes that flow horizontally.

Sheeted / closed pattern is where there's a lot more pattern than background colour. Because these kittens are born with mostly marble pattern visible, humans get excited about seeing what colour is underneath as their cat gets older!

Bulls-eye is not a desired pattern in Bengals. They have a circular marble pattern with a round centre, like a bulls-eye, on the side of them. Because it's very similar to Tabby cats, people aren't a huge fan of this pattern on Bengals.

Silver rosette is another type of colour that a Bengal can be is the silver rosette. Rosettes just means "spots." And when I say spots, I mean spots like a leopard. The cats with these markings look *just like* little snow leopards. Even though Phoenix looks a *little* bit like one, cats with silver rosettes look *exactly* like them. They have a white/silver coat with light grey, dark grey, and black markings.

I have two friends named Lily and Noah that are silver rosettes. They are a little bit lazier than an actual wild cat. They like to lay around on top of their cat house that their human mum bought for them.

Even though they like to lay around, they are just gorgeous. They look like they could be baby snow leopards.

Brown rosette cats look like regular leopards, and actually almost exactly like the Asian leopard cat aside from the differences I told you about in the last chapter. Brown rosettes are so striking. They have a golden coat with brown and dark brown, almost black, rosettes. Their spots are what make them so distinctive.

The last kind of colouring is blue rosette. **Blue rosette** Bengals look just like the other two type of rosette colourings except that their markings are a lot softer. They almost look like a picture of a brown rosette cat that has been edited to be black and white.

The markings are so soft that they make the cat look almost unreal! They have a white coat with light grey to dark grey markings, spots or rosettes all over their bodies!

That's a lot to remember about all of our colours and markings. But don't worry, after you become familiar with Bengal cats, spotting the different kinds and remembering the names for colourings and markings will be as easy as mouse pie.

Types of rosette pattern

(Just to confuse you even more)

Arrowhead rosettes are where the spots appear triangular, with the "tip" of the arrow pointing towards the back of the Bengal's body.

Doughnut rosettes are where the inner spot is almost or completely outlined by a darker colour and the inner spot is a different colour to the background (so three colours total).

Embryonic is where spots show subtle signs of a second colour on the edges (so two and a half colours?)

Cluster rosettes are where small spots of one colour form a cluster around a second coloured inner spot and both spot colours are different from the background colour (so three colours total).

Paw-print rosettes are where the cluster forms around one side of the inner spot, making it look like paw prints running across the background colour (three colours total).

Single-spotting is when the spots have just one colour, so the cats coat comprises of the background colour and the single spot colour (so two colours total).

Long-haired variant

Some Bengals have longer hair. These are Bengals that are F4 generation cats. What that means is that cat is four generations away from the Asian leopard cat. Those cats are completely and totally domesticated.

The long-haired variant of the Bengal has the same markings as the short-haired variant, but they just have longer hair, making them prone to shedding and making them look a little more like a

Maine Coon cat. They have tufts of hair that come out from their neck almost like a lion's mane. The long-haired variant of the Bengal cat is registered as "Cashmere" cats in the New Zealand Cat Fancy.

Bengal cats come in so many varieties! I think that's one of the things that makes us charming and unusual. We are all beautiful in our own ways. All of my Bengal friends are beautiful and so am I.

Glitter

Some Bengals have translucent hair shafts, but a much prettier way of describing it is Bengal glitter! It's usually most visible on our paws or when we're in direct sunlight and it looks like our coats are sparkling. Gold Bengals get gold glitter, snow Bengals get cream-white glitter and silver Bengals get silvery-white glitter. Unfortunately, it's hard to capture in photos, so you'll just have to bask in our beauty in person!

CHAPTER THREE: Personality

Remember when I talked about the F4 long-haired variant of the Bengal cat? And how F4 means four generations removed from the Asian leopard cat? And how that means we're totally domesticated?

Well, you want to make sure that a Bengal you adopt is an F4! That way you ensure that we're totally gentle. That's important especially if you have other animals or small children. A totally domesticated Bengal cat is going to be gentle and tame.

Even though we're tame, we do need a lot of attention. We love being loved on and being played with. One thing we really love to do is play fetch. We can be taught to do tricks on command. All it takes is some time and patience and you can surely get your Bengal to do tricks just like me.

Curiosity (Almost) Killed the Cat

We are extremely curious cats. Some might even say that we're *too* curious. To that I say, whatever do you mean? How else are we supposed to learn about our world?!

Sometimes we can get ourselves into a little bit of trouble with our curiosity. One time my human mum was getting ready for work one morning and I went into the kitchen. No one was around to play with me so I got quite bored. I could smell something in a drawer that was right on my level. I used my little paw to open the drawer and inside I saw some cheese. I hopped on in the drawer and while I was munching on the cheese, the drawer shut.
I started to panic. I meowed really loudly but I knew no one could hear me! I heard the door open and heard my mum start her car to go to work.

I spent the next nine hours in the dark with the block of cheese because I was too curious. Finally, Susan. My human mum came home from work and when I heard her come in, I meowed as loudly as I could. She heard me and rescued me.

"Shirley! How did you get in there?!" she asked me.

I couldn't tell her in human language that it was a mistake, so I just purred and meowed when she picked me up and held me. I'm so attached to Susan. Just seeing her face after such a long day of being all on my own was a huge relief. She has a completely stunning human face, such a gorgeous smile and deep brown eyes, wow, a real stunner for sure. I'm lucky. Sometimes she can be a little stern, but somehow, I even like that?

Anyway, the moral of the story is to always keep your eyes peeled for your Bengal. Before you leave the house, always make sure you know where they are – they could be anywhere! Including in a drawer with a block of cheese.

Smarty Pants

Bengal cats are known for their intelligence. We are extremely curious and extremely smart and something really remarkable about us is that we can be taught to do tricks and be trained! Remember my friend Mystic? Well, she loves to learn new tricks. She has learned how to lie down and roll over on command. Just like a dog, her owner taught her how to do these things with a clicker.

Clicker training is really simple. What you do is teach the cat that the sound of the *click* means that they're doing something right. And to make sure they know that, you give them a treat to reinforce that knowledge. Mystic will lie down and roll over just from hearing the words. After she does these things, her mom gives her a treat to let her know that she's doing things right.

What's That Sound?

Do you hear that? That mewing and crying? That's a Bengal telling you that it's hungry, that it wants to go out, that it's happy, it's sad or it's litter box needs to be cleaned out. The list goes on.

You've guessed it. We are extremely vocal pets. We aren't shy when it comes to expressing our needs to our owners. Sometimes our crying and mewing can get a little out of control but I know my humans adore me for it.

I have a friend from the Netherlands that tends to get loud especially when it gets close to bedtime. Usually, food will calm her down. She screams and meows at her people until they give her a snack or a meal. That's enough to make her happy and get her to be quiet and go to bed. Which brings me to my next topic!

Basically, I'm a huge chatterbox. I like them to know exactly what's happening in my world. I'm quite impressed with myself if truth be told, my sounds vary beyond belief, sometimes I can even say hello, seriously, I'm not joking, in just trying to work out the camera so I can upload it on YouTube...keep a look out.

Other Pets

Some cats aren't very good about interacting with other animals, but that's not the case with Bengals. We love other animals. In fact, my best friend in the world is Pepsi, my standard poodle.

We have lots of adventures together and we love to play. Sometimes Susan, our human, lets us outside. We even compete over who can fetch things, obviously, I win.

For me, it seems that I'm better with dogs than other cats. My best friend Pepsi the Standard Poodle completely adores me, in fact I love her, too, she's like the mum I never had. I follow her everywhere. Her huge nose gets on my nerves sometimes as she pokes around sniffing my fur and inside my ears, but for some reason I just can't bring myself to hiss at her at all. I tried to swipe her yesterday but my claws stayed in. That's how I know I'm just playing with her.

Even my humans wouldn't get in the way to sort out my behaviour with Pepsi. They know that we're just playing. They can tell by my body language.

I used to live with my sister, but unfortunately, she moved next door and deserted us all – *charming*. OK, I may have had a bit of influence on that move. I admit it, I chased her away. So maybe I'm not so great with other cats. Some Bengals are, though. Like my friends Lily and Noah. They live together quite happily. They will

lounge with each other and sometimes they even play together. I don't think I could do it. I much prefer dogs.

Sometimes my territorial nature gets the best of me. Because of that my sister chose the peace and quiet of next door. I'm a little jealous, though, because she gets fed fresh chicken every single day.
There are other Bengals that have trouble interacting with other Bengals or other cats in general. My mum told me about two cats that she read about who couldn't get along. One of the cats was several years old and got along fine with the family's whippet dog. They were great friends. They loved to play and sometimes would get a little rough and tumble with each other, but it was all in good fun.

However, when the family introduced another cat – a Bengal kitten – into the home, the other cat started having problems. The older cat would growl and hiss at the younger kitten and sometimes it would pin the kitten down and try to bite it, and not in a playful way.

These are important things to keep in mind when you're thinking about adopting a second cat into your home. It might not be the best experience for either cat and eventually the new cat might need a new home. You wouldn't want to have to put a cat through that.

Temperament

Remember when I talked about the F4 long-haired variant of the Bengal cat? And how F4 means four generations removed from the Asian leopard cat? And how that means we're totally domesticated?

Well, you want to make sure that a Bengal you adopt is an F4. That way you are more likely to ensure that we're totally gentle. That's important especially if you have other animals or small children. A totally domesticated Bengal cat is going to be gentle and tame.

Even though we're tame, we do need a lot of attention. We love being loved and being played with. Basically, we adore attention. One thing we really love to do is play fetch. I play fetch with a rolled-up piece of tin foil, just love it. We can be taught to do tricks on command. All it takes is some time and patience and you can surely get your Bengal to do tricks just like me.

Behaviours

Are Bengals troublemakers?

Of course, we aren't.

Okay...

Maybe we are. A little bit. This goes back to our curious nature. Sometimes we can get ourselves into a little bit of trouble, just like I did when I got trapped with the block of cheese.

Bengals don't go looking for trouble, but we have been known for it to find us. Sometimes we can fight with other animals or cause problems because our personalities can clash with those other animals.

It's something to consider strongly before adding a Bengal cat to your household if you already have other pets. But like I said before, Pepsi and I get along great. No rule is hard and fast for all Bengals, but most of them can be applied to most Bengals.

Remember that we're all individuals. Don't label us. Try not to judge us and the world will be a happier place.

While Bengal's are no more or less prone to behavioural problems than any other cat, we can sometimes be bullies. I'm not proud to admit that about our beautiful breed, but we can be territorial with other cats. I know some cats who completely terrorise the other cats who live with them, and some even go out of their way to harass the neighbourhood cats.

I don't associate with these brutes; I've been taught better. If your Bengal is being a bit of a bully, it might be a good idea to try these behaviour therapy techniques.

If your Bengal is intimidating another cat in your household, try putting a bell on the Bengal's collar so that they can't sneak up on your unsuspecting feline friend. This will give your other cat a much-needed heads up on the Bengal's presence so it can't be startled by a surprise attack.

Another idea might be to section off areas of your house so that your cats don't have to be in close quarters of each other. Bengal's are very territorial, so sometimes they just need their own space that is solely for them. Lots of Bengal's humans invest in mesh doors or gates so that cats can see each other without getting into each other's' space. This not only gives them each their own territories, but also allows them to get used to each other without any risk of fighting.

Fortunately, because we're such a smart breed, we take to training very quickly.

Spraying

Spraying can be an issue with any breed of cat. It may be behavioural, or it could indicate an underlying health problem such as a UTI. Spraying is the most common behavioural problem exhibited by Bengal cats, and it can be resolved with patience and determination.

If and when you first notice that your Bengal has been spraying, the first thing you should do it consult your vet to make sure it isn't happening because of medical reasons. We'll go over this in more detail in Chapter Seven: Health and Welfare.

Once you've ruled out any medical issues, there are several behavioural reasons why your cat might be spraying.

Stress

There are several methods you can try to reduce stress, and hopefully spraying, in your cat.

Pet rescue remedy is an all-natural solution that calms your cat down by adding a couple of drops to their food. You can find various brands on Amazon or at your local pet store.

Alternatively, you could try **Zylkene** (also available on Amazon) if your Bengal is still a kitten. Zylkene has a milk compound similar to that found in a mother's milk which calms kittens.

The third option is to invest in a **Feliway diffuser or spray**. Feliway is the leading cat behaviour product in the UK, scientifically proven to help stop and prevent unwanted behaviours in cats. It mimics the pheromone that cats create when we feel safe.

Territory

Like I said before, we can be very territorial. If there's a cat outside who we perceive to be a threat, we may spray to mark our territory. The easiest way to tell if this is the case with your spraying Bengal is to look at **where the spraying is occurring**. If we are marking our territory from an outdoor cat, we are likely to spray onto the window or on the wall near the window. The risk with an indoor cat feeling territorial over an outdoor cat is that your Bengal may lash out at the other pets in your home. If you have a female cat and she is unspayed, that could be what is drawing the attention of the male outdoor cats. It might also be that the outdoor cat(s) has access to food in your garden, maybe from bird feeders you have set up or catnip you may be growing in our garden.

So here are some methods to try if territory is the issue

A possible solution here is to prevent us from being able to see the outdoor cat, whether by **blocking views to the outside** or by **putting deterrents into your garden** (assuming your Bengal doesn't go out there).

Some popular deterrents include **citrus fruit peel**, such as oranges, lemons or limes, which you can toss into the garden. Cats don't like strong citrus smells! The risk with fruit peel is that you might attract other wild animals into your garden who aren't as fussy. You can **empty your hairbrush** out into the garden – cats are put off by human hair and it will help you to reclaim your territory.

Be sure to avoid putting moth balls outside, though, as they're toxic to cats and humans. If the outside cat is coming into your garden to use it as a giant litterbox, you could try placing some **garden mesh or chicken wire** just underneath the top layer of soil. We like to scratch and dig when we go to the bathroom, and the layer of mesh will make this difficult. You can even cut holes into it where your plants need to go.

This suggestion may seem a little mean, but desperate times call for desperate measures. You could always get a **motion-activated sprinkler** for your garden. Make sure you don't put it some place that people walk around, and it probably won't work if the outside cat is a Bengal! But other cats aren't the biggest fans of water and will soon learn to avoid your garden!

Litter Box

Your cat may be spraying because it has issues with the litter box. If you are **cleaning your cat's litterbox** thoroughly, it won't smell of cat anymore and we're less willing to do our business there. You can use a scoop to clean out the box daily, keeping it dry and poo-free, Bengal's are very picky about having a clean bathroom! But, you should avoid washing it too regularly – it's important to leave a bit of cat scent!

It might be that your cat doesn't like **the type of litter** you're using, or the box itself. Some of us like a little privacy, and a box with a lid is ideal, and some of us like plenty of room. You should figure out which your Bengal prefers!

You may not have enough litter boxes in your home. The golden ratio is **1 litter boxes per cat, plus 1 extra**. So, if you have one cat, you need two litter boxes; two cats, three litter boxes. Some of us like to pee in one box and poo in another, but some of us just like having **our own litter box**.

Some easy ways to tell if this is the case

Going to the bathroom outside of the litter box, if medical conditions are ruled out, may be an indication from your Bengal that they're unhappy with their litter box situation. If you have a multi-cat home and your Bengal is spraying on the outside of the box, or leaving their pee/poo uncovered, that's an indication that they're marking it as their own and you should probably invest in another.

Litter boxes should be **kept in a different room** to where you set down our food, or at least 4 feet away - we don't like to poo where we eat!

Scent Marking

It's vital that you properly clean the area if your Bengal sprays where it isn't supposed to. While you humans may not be able to see the stains, or smell any residual scent after using standard household cleaner, cat urine is very potent so you can bet that we can still smell it. My human, Susan, says that many people who have Bengals highly recommend a product called *Urine Off*, which you can get on Amazon. It's very good at getting the job done!

If your Bengal is marking your bed, it's a good idea to **restrict their access** to the bedroom until their spraying issues are resolved. Then you can begin to reintroduce them to the area under supervision. In order to mark your cats scent on areas (without the gross mess) rub their cheeks with your hands and then rub your hands onto the desired marking area. This may reduce their desire to spray the area!

Alternatively, you can **buy cheap plastic sheets** to cover your bed or sofa until the spraying ceases. A cheap plastic shower curtain may be deterrent enough, or you could get rolls of plastic or tarp that you would traditionally be used to protect your floor/furniture while painting!

I have a friend called Adam (left), who lives with his brother Splash (right) in America. They aren't Bengals, but they're still pretty cool. Adam recently started to go to the bathroom on his human's bed! His human, Caroline, still isn't sure why he's doing it, but while she's figuring it out she's using plastic painting sheets to cover her bed while she goes to work! Maybe I should send Caroline a copy of this book, my toilet tips might be useful!

It's important that you **do not to shout at your cat** if it goes to the toilet someplace other than their litter box. Cats don't understand shouting and it will just stress them out further.

You can also try what I like to call the **Bengal Rain Dance**; if you dig in your cat's litter box (make sure it's clean first!) it's exactly like when humans hear running water and suddenly need to use the bathroom. Digging in your kitty's litter might encourage them to go.

Lady's in Heat: It's important to note that if you're breeding your Bengal, most **females will spray when they're in heat** – especially if

you have other lady cats in your house. A lot of people seem to think only male cats spray, but us ladies are just as guilty!

Attention

So maybe I have some attachment issues. So what?

I clearly have a problem. It's not my fault, though. I was locked in a cage for six months. Now I finally have a forever home so I shouldn't have to worry about that sort of thing, but sometimes our past traumas don't go away very easily. I need stability and I need routine. Almost any cat (or dog) that has lived in a shelter or a bad situation will feel this way. I need my humans to play with me all the time and adore me.

Not all Bengals are the same, but that's how it is for me. Most of my friends are pretty settled. My friend Alfred is incredibly confident. He doesn't need hardly any reassurance of his place in his house at all.

That's not always the case, though.

Many of us get quite attached to our humans and need their reassurance whenever they can give it. This means that if you get a Bengal cat, be sure to be ready to give them lots of love and affection. They're going to want it and need it.

Some people think of cats and think of the phrase, "as independent as a cat" Don't think of that phrase when you think about me; I can be very dependent sometimes, and so can a lot of my friends. You'll just have to see what kind of personality your Bengal cat has.

Bed Time

Just remember, a bed isn't just for sleeping in.

My little friend from the Netherlands is a perfect example of how crazy we can get at bedtime. She runs around and around and drives her parents absolutely insane. Her mom asked some of my mom's friends if it was normal for her to be acting so mad!

Of course it is.

Sometimes we Bengals can have "normal" behaviours for us that are not so normal for other types of cats.

Sometimes when we cry for attention at night time, what we want is food, just like my friend that I mentioned. Other times we're wanting to play, but sometimes playing at night can have the opposite effect of what you want it to.

It seems like it would tire us out, right?

Well, sometimes our bodies can be just like a person's body. If you exercise late at night, it might make you sleepy, but there's a good chance that it will hype you up and make it nearly impossible to lay down and get some good rest.

Keep that in mind when taking care of your Bengal at night.

It's best to get into a steady routine with your Bengal at bedtime. Just like children, we will adjust to the routine that you set for them. Beware, though, we can be quite stubborn and are very intelligent. Don't try to trick us into going to bed.

Leave water out for us at night (and really, all the time). It's important for any pet to have access to water at all times. We could get dehydrated and end up quite sick if we don't get the right amount of water. By leaving out water at night or making sure that our water dishes are full, you're ensuring that we won't wake you up for water, at least.

We still might wake you up for something else, though. We're quite mischievous.

Here's a great one. I don't know if it's just me that does this but my favourite game when it rains at night, I bring worms in throughout the night (and put them on my human's face). Needless to say, the humans are ever too impressed with this game...

CHAPTER FOUR: Food

Water

The rumours are true – Bengals love water. I ADORE water. Like our namesake, the Bengal cat loves water just as much as the Bengal tiger.

If you have a pond or a pool, don't be surprised if your Bengal can be spotted from time to time splashing around in it with its paws or exploring the edges of the pond looking in at the fish. Sometimes we think that we're actually wild cats like a tiger.

I have to admit, when my mum has a bath, I just can't stop playing with the water, I'm just fascinated – it's not very relaxing for her though, hee hee, but I love it!!!! I especially love dipping my tail in the water, sometimes I even try and eat the bubbles. Dipping our paws into the bath feels lovely, so don't run the water too hot or we might burn our little paw beans!

A lot of Bengal's don't like their water to be too close to their food, so it's best to place our water down in a secondary location (or multiple places, if you have more than one cat).

Diet and Feeding

While dogs can sometimes be fed vegetarian diets (usually because of medical conditions) and remain healthy, us cats are carnivores and we need meat in our diets. Something important to check when you're buying us our kibble is to make sure the first ingredient is meat. Lots of brands of kibble have corn, corn gluten or by-products as their main ingredient, and we just aren't about that life. Taking some extra time to find us a grain-free cat food will reduce the chances of our tummies getting upset, and we'll be a lot happier as a result!

While meat is the most important ingredient in a Bengal's diet, we also need vitamins and minerals to balance things out, and making sure we get a good amount of all three is really important! Protein should make up around 50%-80% of our diets, leaving plenty of room for fibre and vitamins! A cat has to keep her figure, after all. I've included a very useful measuring system so that you can figure out how much food to give your cat based on how much they weigh. Make sure to use scales rather than guessing though (remember, these are only estimations)

12-week old kitten (approx.)	**110 calories per pound daily**
16-week old kitten (approx.)	**80 calories per pound daily**
24-week old kitten (approx.)	**60-70 calories per pound daily**
40-week old kitten (approx.)	**35-45 calories per pound daily**
Intact adult cat (approx.)	**30 calories per pound daily**
Spayed/neutered adult cat (approx.)	**26 calories per pound daily**
Overweight adult cat (approx.)	**18-22 calories per pound daily**

Raw Diet

Because we are so closely related to wild cats, it's not unusual that many humans consider feeding us raw meat. The raw diet is widely debated among humans, but let me tell you how to decide whether to try it or not, cat to person. First of all, talk to your cat, see what they think, give them a bit of chicken wing – I was so excited with my first taste. You could even talk to your vet. Don't get me wrong, I'm not a huge fan of going to the vet, (what cat is?) *but* they do sometimes know what they're talking about. Personally, I adore my RAW food, but many of my friends prefer to mix it up.

You also need to keep in mind that feeding us solely raw meat isn't going to give us a balanced diet. We also need vitamins and minerals, which you can give us supplements for, but this can be tiresome for you humans and so you may consider just giving us additional types of food to balance things out.

Secondly, consider your cat's current diet. We get pretty comfortable with our feeding habits, so switching our diets up out of nowhere can be really confusing for us. If you are keen on starting your Bengal on a raw diet, then you need to introduce it slowly. Alternatively, if you've got a Bengal that is used to a raw diet and you want to wean it off and onto standard cat food, this change should also be made slowly.

The third, and most important thing, is to make sure you are safe. If you have taken all of the above steps and arrive at the conclusion that your cat is going to eat raw meat for at least a portion of their diet, then you need to be cautious. Don't give us huge portions of raw meat. We would only hunt small game in the wild, so over-feeding us can upset our tummies! Don't leave any meat out for longer than 20 minutes – if we don't eat it, throw it away. Room temperature meat can make us ill if it's left out for too long! It's also important to thoroughly clean our bowls in between meals.

You also shouldn't feed kittens raw meat, because Salmonella can kill young kittens. So, if you have another young kitten in your household, take into consideration how you're going to reduce the risk of contamination. Especially since we like to lick each other!

As well as this, you need to make sure the meat you do give to your cat is of a high quality. You can buy commercially prepared raw diet materials, which can save you some of the work here, or you can take the time to grind up meat for us yourself – but be sure to check it's fresh and not processed, and remember to take sanitisation into consideration!

My friend Janice will only eat at the table with her human, Donna. If Donna stops eating her meal and starts removing the dishes, Janice stops eating too! The only way she will eat if Donna stays with her while she eats. If she is served her meal in the morning before Donna prepares hers, Janice won't touch hers until Donna sits down and start eating too. Sounds like good manners to me!

Another friend, Snickers, was obsessed with licking the blood from her raw chicken, but her human was worried it might be bad for her. So, they worked together to revise her diet, and now she eats one meal of quail, one meal rabbits' meat, one meal of seafood and one meal of organs with supplements. Her favourite is chicken liver!

A lot of my Bengal friends prefer turkey to chicken, but personally, I love raw chopped up chicken wings – they're so yummy! I've noticed that it is a bit of a challenge for my human because she's a vegan. The fact that she'll handle my raw meat treat just goes to show that she really does love me!

Absolute No-No's

Since I've taken it upon myself to educate you humans, I've got to provide you with the facts about what you should never feed to your Bengals – even though we might still *try* to get a taste because we're curious and don't know any better. So, it's *your* job to make sure we don't get our paws on any of the following:

Avocado – I know that avocados have become strangely popular amongst you humans recently, but they contain persin, which is a highly toxic substance for us felines!

Alcohol – this can be fatal for your cat, causing brain or liver damage as well as being highly intoxicating. It doesn't matter if it's beer, wine, or food that has alcohol in it, we can't have it.

Cooked Bones – These can splinter and we might choke on bones, or block or slice at our intestines.

Caffeine – this is extremely toxic to cats, especially in large quantities. No tea, coffee or fizzy drinks for us.

Chocolate – like my poodle friend, I'm not allowed chocolate. It contains theobromine which is highly poisonous for us. If it's not taken care off quickly, then theobromine poisoning can be fatal!

Liver – in small quantities, liver is fine. But too much can cause a vitamin A toxicity which affects our bones.

Macadamia nuts – these nuts are rich in fat, which can cause us stomach upset, resulting in vomiting or diarrhoea. No cat wants that.

Raw eggs – not only do raw eggs risk us getting salmonella, but raw egg whites can cause skin and coat problems.

Raw potatoes / tomatoes – both of these have glycoalkaloid solanine in them, which can give us digestive illnesses.

Xylitol – your sweets, snacks, chewing gum and baked goods contain a sweetener called Xylitol which can cause a fast blood sugar drop in your Bengal.

Yeast dough – because yeast ferments produce alcohol, we aren't allowed it for the same reason we can't have alcohol: alcohol poisoning.

Food for the Ages

Cats are a lot like people in that our diets change as we age. I'll go into more detail in *Chapter Nine: The Bengal Kitten* and *Chapter Ten: The Elderly Bengal*, but it's important for you to know that you should be looking at age-specific foods for your Bengal throughout their lives. For example, canned food is easier to digest for old or sick Bengals, and you shouldn't give raw meat to kittens.

When you first get your Bengal and bring them home, it's important that you maintain the diet that they're used to. Immediate changes can cause us upset tummies. Once your Bengal is entirely settled in to their new home, you can begin to gradually change their diet if you want by slowly incorporating the new food in with their regular food and gradually increasing the amount of new food while decreasing the amount of old food.

The Milk Myth

I've noticed that a lot of humans think that cats drink milk. Don't get me wrong, we like milk, but it's not particularly healthy for us. You shouldn't give us your people-milk because it's too high in lactose which can be bad for us. If you do think we deserve a treat, you should buy milk especially made for kittens and cats (check your pet store or the pet aisle in the supermarket) and give us that on special occasions!

If your cat has a balanced diet, then they don't need to rely on milk as a source of nutrition. But, again, we do like milk (the for-cats kind) and letting us have some every now and then is perfectly fine!

Nothing can replace our love for water though!

CHAPTER FIVE: Play Time

You probably already know that cats love to play – pieces of string, laser pointers, and all sorts of other things we can get our tiny paws on. We Bengals, though, take play time to a whole new level!

It's play time *all* the time!

Bengals can jump approximately 4 feet into the air – so even if you think you've put something out of reach, chances are we can still get to it. It also means that we really like high spaces. Don't be too surprised if you find us sitting on top of the door frames! It's a good idea to make some high places for us to perch and overlook our territory. You can buy a really tall cat tree, or even just make some gaps on a tall bookshelf for us to lounge about on!

When my human takes Pepsi out for walks, I like to tag along. What? I don't like being left out! Because we live in a very rural area with lots of fields, I'm allowed to venture outside and it's perfectly safe for me. So, when my two best friends go for a stroll, you can bet I'll be trotting along beside them.

Remember in Chapter Three when I told you about how smart we Bengal's are? Well, we're so smart we can learn (and love) to play fetch. I have another kitty friend named Leo. He absolutely loves to play fetch just like I do! He will play with a small ball or with a toy shaped like a mouse or a bird. Just like a dog he will wait for his parents to throw the toy and then he will run after it, pick it up, and bring it back to play all over again.

Some people are stunned by the Bengal cat's ability to learn tricks and to play fetch, but I just can't imagine why anyone would be surprised, since we're so smart.

I love being told what a good girl I am. And one of the best ways for my human to do that with me is to engage in some training with rewards.

Rewards don't always have to be treats, and it's probably healthier for your Bengal if they aren't always rewarded with a treat. They might get fat and unhealthy that way.

Some cats are food-motivated and others are attention-motivated. You have to figure out which type of motivation works with your cat, first of all.

Some type of reward system works with training just about any animal. Aside from rewards, there's one other thing that you're going to need...

Clicker

You can purchase a clicker at your local pet shop or online somewhere like Amazon. There are some that come with a stretchable band that allows you to keep the clicker on your wrist and easy to access but allowing your hands to remain free.

After you've bought a clicker, you're probably going to want to know how clicker training works.

Clicker training, at its very most basic form, is positive reinforcement. When an action is commanded by the human, if the animal performs the action, the clicker is clicked and a treat, toy, or affection is given to let the cat know that what they have done is good.

It's a lot like Pavlov's dog. If you know anything about psychology, you know that there were some dogs that he conditioned to understand that when they heard a bell ring, food was going to be coming their way. The dogs got to the point where they would salivate just at the ringing of the bell even if the food hadn't shown up yet. The same principle applies to clicker training.

Really, it's quite simple and easy to get the hang of for both the owner and the Bengal cat.

Tricks

You'll probably want to start out with some basic things like "come," "sit," and "stay." But once you've mastered these commands and others like, "leave it" for when a cat has something they shouldn't have, you can move on to more impressive and fancy tricks.

I told you earlier about my friend who does lots of tricks! There are videos on YouTube of my friend and of other Bengals performing tricks on command.

Cats can be taught to fetch and to roll over, just like a dog. They can be taught to shake and to speak. All it takes is patience and dedication to training.

The best way to teach a cat to roll over is to teach them to lie down, first.

After they are lying down, take the toy or the treat and bring it around the back of the cat's neck, making the cat look for it. When it becomes too much of a strain to look for the toy or treat that way, the cat will naturally roll onto its back. After you've gotten them to that position, keep pulling the treat or toy away from them until they roll back into the lying position.

Voila.

You've taught your Bengal how to roll over! Isn't it easy?! This technique works with dogs, as well.

To teach your Bengal to shake, you use the toy or treat as motivation and start by placing your hand behind their front leg. Push it forward after you say "shake" and continue until they are in the desired position for shaking their paw. After that, try to push on the leg less and less until the Bengal is raising their leg on their own.

Now you've got two fancy tricks in your routine! Get ready to amaze your friends with your trained Bengal cat!

Really, when it comes to clicker training, the sky is the limit.

Toys

We Bengals love our toys. If you humans think that you've played with a cat, you don't know what you're talking about! Playing with a Bengal is an entirely different thing.

Something important to note, though: you should always use toys when you're playing with us. It's for the best that we aren't taught to associate your hands and feet as targets. We'd feel terrible if we ever hurt you!

I just told you that we love to play fetch. And we do. Our favourite toys are often balls, mouse-shaped toys, and bird-shaped toys. To be honest though, I love nothing better than a wine cork, a rolled-up bit of tin foil or a screwed-up shop receipt.

Sometimes I get tired of my toys and they end up in the rubbish bin. It's good to go through your cat's toys every once in a while, and throw out whatever the cat doesn't like to play with anymore.

There is a toy that you can buy on Amazon for your kitty that's called Skitter Critters. They are mouse-shaped catnip toys. I'm not keen but my friends love them. The mice have catnip in them, which everyone knows will drive a cat *CRAZY!* I love them! You Bengal will love fetching them and will roll all around the floor playing with them day after day.

There's another toy called Da'Bird. I love that thing, ADORE IT. It's a stick with some feathers attached to the end. Your Bengal will absolutely love it too I'm sure. You can trail it around the room, walking in front of your Bengal or sit right on the couch and pull it up and down in the air, getting your Bengal to leap after it. It's guaranteed hours of fun for you and your pet.

When it comes to finding the right toy for your Bengal, it will just take a little bit of time.

You'll know when you find something that your cat truly enjoys. Don't be afraid to buy several toys to see which one your Bengal enjoys the most. As I said though, I'm easy and cheap, give me screwed up pieces of paper and tin foil and I'm yours. So, pleasing your cat might be as simple as that. You don't have to worry about spending a lot of money.

CHAPTER SIX: Grooming

The Bengal breed's grooming habits are slightly different to other cats. Because of this, their grooming habits require some slightly different rules, but don't worry, I'm going to tell you exactly how it's done.

> Fun Fact: Bengal cats shed considerably less than other cats – some humans even insist we don't shed at all!

Brushing

Some things to take into account when considering your Bengal's grooming schedule:

- **Bengals self-groom a lot more than other breeds – we like to make sure we always look our absolute best! Vanity, who, _me_?**

- **While we are considered hypoallergenic, our saliva has a protein that contributes to humans' cat allergies, brushing us more frequently may spark these allergies.**

- **A lot of humans like to brush their Bengal friends once a week or so. They say this keeps our coats healthy and minimises our already limited shedding!**

Now that I've given you some context and some suggestions on how often to brush us, let's get into the technical details of _how_ to brush us...

When brushing your Bengal, or any cat, you should always brush _with_ the coat. We were all witness to that weird backcombing human phase and we weren't impressed. You should also use a metal tooth comb that is specifically designed for cats. While we might like a number of other brushes, a metal tooth comb is best for removing dirt, tangled or matted fur, and I *personally* think it feels really nice along my cheeks.

Nail Trimming

A lot of the time, your cat's nails will shed naturally. You shouldn't be surprised or concerned if you find old claw sheaths around your cat's scratching posts or on their cat trees. It's a lot like snakes shedding their skin!

If your cat's nails do get long and you aren't confident in clipping them yourself, you can take them to a groomer or the vet. Alternatively, you can do them yourself by following my super great advice...

It's important to make sure you have the **right tools**. You need to make sure you have cat specific nail clippers, and you may also want a styptic pencil or styptic powder.

The **best time** to trim your cat's nails is when they're calm and comfortable. Either when they've just had a yummy meal or have woken up from a nice, relaxing nap.

It's important to **give us a treat afterwards** as positive reinforcement. We don't just sit still without there being something in it for us!

You use the nail clippers to trim the edge of your cat's claws, but make sure you don't nick the quick!

The quick is the pink bit of the cat's claws. It's made up of nerve endings and blood vessels, so it hurts if you clip it!

If you're having trouble finding where your cat's quick begins, try shining a light on the claws and you should be able to see it a little clearer!

It's better to not clip enough nail than to accidentally get the quick. If you do accidentally snip the quick, that's when you'd use the styptic pencil.

A styptic pencil can be found in most pharmacies, and they help to cauterize the blood vessels by touching the pencil to the nail if it starts bleeding. If you cut your cat's quick, hold the pencil to the nail for **one or two minutes** to stop the bleeding.

If you don't have any styptic products to hand, my there are some home remedies you can try:

Pack the nail with flour. Make sure your cat stays still for a few minutes while you pack the nail so the flour can absorb the bleeding and help the blood to clot. Corn starch might also work if you have no flour.

A bar of soap. Scrape the nail against the bar until it becomes packed with soap.

Elevate the paw. Just like you would with a human, raise your cat's paw into the air above heart level to slow the bleeding.

In the event that you do cut the quick, the bleeding should stop within **five to seven minutes**. If it doesn't show signs of letting up, you should contact your vet immediately.

De-clawing

A lot of humans have a lot of misconceptions about de-clawing. They think it equates to trimming your nails down or getting a manicure.

Let me tell you what de-clawing really is, and then, hopefully, you'll understand why it's an absolute no-no.

What a lot of humans don't know is that scratching is actually healthy behaviour for a cat. We scratch so that we can exercise our muscles, maintain our claws, and because it's a lot of fun! This is why cat owners invest in scratching posts – so we can have all the fun and health benefits of scratching without destroying your furniture!

Now, let me lay down some truths about de-clawing...

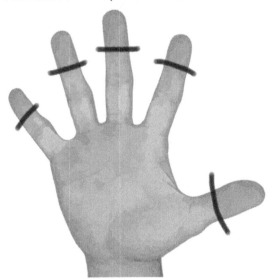

De-clawing a cat is the same as **amputating the first digit** of each of your fingers.

A de-clawed cat will wake up from surgery in pain, and that pain will continue even after they have "healed".

Claws can re-grow inside our paws which causes extreme pain that humans can't see.

We have to re-learn how to walk after de-clawing. Our nails are crucial to our balance, not unlike if you suddenly had no toes.

A de-clawed cat is more likely to become aggressive post-surgery, because without our claws we feel very insecure and so we're more likely to bite as a means of defence. They are also more likely to start doing their business outside of the litterbox (even if they're perfectly house trained) as a way of marking territory.

What to do instead of de-clawing

Now that you're aware of how barbaric de-clawing is, here are some things you can implement to prevent your cat from scratching where they aren't supposed to...

Trim your cat's nails regularly.

I've already explained how to trim your cat's claws earlier in this chapter. By removing the hook of your cat's nails basically removes the ability for the claws to do any real damage.

Buy several scratching posts.

The ideal scratching post is at least 3 feet tall (so we can really stretch out) and is made of rough material. Those fluffy carpeted scratching posts just won't cut it, because they won't meet our scratching needs. You should have at least 2 sturdy scratching posts in your home.

Teach us where to scratch.

By sprinkling a little cat nip on our scratching posts once a week, we will be much more motivated to use them! If you notice we like to scratch specific pieces of your furniture, maybe move our scratching posts so that they are nearby as an acceptable alternative. If you catch us scratching some place we aren't supposed to, carry your cat to the scratching post and encourage them to use that instead.

CHAPTER SEVEN: Health & Welfare

There's a lot more to looking after your cat than remembering to feed them. Just like humans, we need good nutrition, exercise and to maintain a healthy weight.

The best way to look out for the welfare of your cat is to put preventative health care measures in place. It only makes sense to give us the proper tools to defend ourselves against disease, illness and parasites.

Lifespan

A healthy Bengal will live for around 10-16 years. Indoor cats have been known to live as long as 20 years, though.

A cat's lifespan can depend on numerous factors; lifestyle, diet, exercise, and the overall health of their breed.

So, while our lifespan depends on the individual cat, as a human, you need to be prepared to share your life with your feline friend for at least a decade.

Sleep

As I've mentioned previously, we Bengal cats are a very active breed. Lots of humans wonder if we ever sleep at all! Because we require so much stimulation, our sleeping habits generally depend on how much energy we burn off over the course of the day.

A lot of domestic cats will sleep for around 16 hours a day, usually in very cute positions that humans like to take pictures of. As we get older, it's not surprising for us to sleep as much as 20 hours a day.

Bengal cats, though, average around 12 to 14 hours of sleep per day, because our natural inclination to explore and play is a lot higher than other cats. Plus, when our humans are at home, how can we sleep when we can play with them?

While every cat's sleep schedule will vary based on their individual lifestyle, if you notice your cat is sleeping significantly more or less than they usually would it might be a red flag that something is wrong.

If your cat begins to sleep a whole lot **more** than they usually do, this might be a sign that they're in pain or suffering from illness. Rather than chalk it up to nothing, it's a good idea to contact your vet.

If you have noticed your cat is sleeping **less** than normal, it could be because of other problems such as hyperthyroidism (a common glandular disorder).

Other symptoms include excessive thirst, urinating more frequently, hyperactivity, unkempt appearance, panting, diarrhoea and increased shedding. The most common symptoms, however, are weight loss and vomiting. Hyperthyroidism is mostly found in older cats, and can be treated with medication, surgery, or radioactive iodine therapy (injections).

Fun Fact: Three quarters of the time, when your cat is sleeping they're really just dozing. This allows them to remain alert and wake up at a moment's notice if they need to. The other quarter of the time, they're in a deep cat sleep and can even have cat dreams!

Preventative health care

Cats aren't exactly able to tell their humans when they're sick, and even if they were, it's not worth having to see your cat suffering when you could have done something to prevent it. Preventative health care is crucial if you want your cat to live a long, happy life.

You can often get healthcare packages from your vet that offer varying treatments depending on your cat's age and lifestyle.

Vaccination:

Vaccines can protect your cat from major infectious diseases, and it's important to keep them up to date so that they remain effective. If you get your Bengal as a new born kitten, their first vaccine should be when they are 9 weeks old. The first round of vaccines are usually carried out across several weeks, ending when your kitten reaches around 16 weeks.

Once you have vaccinated your cat as a kitten, it is crucial for you to take your cat for regular booster vaccinations, otherwise they may be at risk. Regardless of whether you decide to keep your cat indoors or not, kitten vaccinations are very important to carry out.

On average, cats should receive booster shots every 3 years, though many humans with indoor cats wait between 5 and 7 years.

Neutering:

It is strongly advised that you spay or neuter your cat. This isn't even just so you can prevent accidental kittens, but there are many health benefits. Female cats can't get uterine cancer, are less likely to get urinary tract infections and their risk of mammary cancer goes down by 25% if they have been spayed. Make cats that have been neutered can't get testicular cancer and have been proven to live 40% longer than unneutered males.

If you are hesitant to spay or neuter your cat because you're interested in breeding your Bengal (which I'll go over more in Chapter Eleven), then I get it. Bengals are great. But, there is also an overpopulation of cats in both the UK and the US.

In 2014, the RSPCA declared that the UK was in a full-on cat crisis, pointing out that there are 30,000 unwanted cats showing up in shelters every year. And what's worse, is that the number of cats being adopted is decreasing.

So, as a cat who was lucky enough to be adopted from a shelter, I'd like to ask that you please seriously consider spaying or neutering your cat, and look into your local shelters and see if they have the perfect Bengal for you.

Fleas:

Because we eat a lot of the fleas they have while grooming ourselves, it can be difficult to tell if your cat even has fleas. Seeing your cat scratching or getting flea bites yourself might be the only way you would notice!

A great trick for checking for fleas is to stand your cat on a piece of plain white paper, and then run a flea comb through their coat and see if any flea dirt (that's the nice way of saying flea poo) comes off onto the paper. If you do notice any small black specs, get some damp cotton wool and dab the dirt with it. If it is flea dirt, it will slowly dissolve and leave red-brown blood marks. Then you know your poor beautiful Bengal cat has fleas.

Now that you know your cat has fleas, here's what you need to do.

First, treat your cat for the fleas. There are numerous flea treatments available, but it is better to get something prescription strength from your vet.

Vacuum all the floors, soft furnishing, gaps between floorboards, difficult to reach places and cat tree platforms and then immediately empty out the hoover. Once you have vacuumed, use a suitable flea insecticide to kill anything you might have missed.

You should also wash any bedding, blankets, and your own bed covers to kill off any fleas that drop off your cat or who had fallen off before treatment.

It is best to contact your vet and ask them the best ways to treat your infestation.

Once you have handled the infestation, you should consider preventative flea control. If you have no pets that go outside, it is unlikely that you will need any further flea treatment. However, if you do have outdoor animals, you will need to invest in regular flea treatment to be safe. Tackling fleas on a one-off basis isn't ideal because they are hard to spot in the first place, and it provides the ideal conditions for your animal to develop flea allergic skin disease.

Worming:

It's also really difficult to tell if your cat has worms. We really don't make it easy for our humans! Some symptoms that might display if your cat has worms include weight loss, vomiting, diarrhoea, irritation around the anus and failure to thrive, i.e. insufficient weight gain or inappropriate weight loss.

There are several types of worms your cat might contract.

Roundworms are very common in kittens, as they can become infected by their mother's milk. Because of this, kittens should be assumed to have worms and be treated regardless at a young age. Kittens should be treated every 2 weeks from the time they are 3 weeks old to 8 weeks old, and then treated monthly until they are 6 months old. Adult cats (older than 6 months) should be treated every 1-3 months.

Tapeworms are normally only an issue for older cats, but kittens can get them if they also have fleas. Adult cats (6 months+) should be treated every 1-3 months with a treatment suitable for combatting both tapeworms and roundworms. Treatment effective against flea tapeworms should be used on kittens.

These are just the two most common kinds of worms your cat might contract, so it's important to remain vigilant and keep an eye on any other potentially infected areas.

When it comes to choosing which product to use to fight off worms, it is best to first consult your vet.

FIV: Feline Immunodeficiency Virus

Cats who have FIV might not even know about it until years after the original infection. It's a slow-acting virus and it lowers the immune system, opening us up to a variety of secondary infections.

If a cat is known to have FIV, they ought to be kept indoors and provided with a stress-free environment. Many cats with FIV can go on to live for several years provided they are suitably taken care of!

FIV is passed on from cat to cat through deep bite wounds. These often occur in outdoor male cats who get into intense fights with others, and is one of the reasons a lot of humans choose to keep their cats indoors. FIV can also be passed from FIV-positive mothers to her kittens. However, kittens who do test FIV positive should be re-tested after they reach about 6 months old, since during that time their mother's antibodies may have cleared out of their systems.

FIV Fact: humans can't contract FIV. It can only be passed from cat to cat, not cat to human.

The symptoms of FIV may present sporadically, or build gradually. These symptoms include enlarged lymph nodes, fever, anaemia, weight loss, dishevelled coat, poor appetite, diarrhoea, conjunctivitis, gingivitis, mouth inflammation, dental disease, redness of skin or hair loss, wounds that won't heal, sneezing, discharge from eyes or nose, frequent urination, straining to urinate or urinating outside of litter box, changes in behaviour. If your cat presents any of these symptoms, it is important to get them in to see the vet as soon as possible.

If you suspect your cat has FIV, it is imperative to keep them indoors and away from any other cats in order to prevent the infection from spreading.

FIV is diagnosed with blood tests, and while there is no cure, it is treatable. This is done with medication for secondary infections, providing a healthy, palatable diet to encourage good nutrition, fluid and electrolyte replacement therapy, anti-inflammatory drugs, immune-enhancing drugs and parasite control.

Once you have a diagnosis, you should take care of your FIV positive cat by **keeping them indoors** to protect them from getting any further disease and to prevent the infection from spreading to the other cats in your area.

You should **keep a close eye on your cat's health** and behaviour, even changes that seem small can be cause for concern, and you should report any worries to your vet.

Speaking of the vet, you should take your cat for **twice annual check-ups** to assess their overall health, blood count and urine tests.

It's important to feed your cat a **balanced, nutritional diet**. FIV cats should **not be given a raw food diet**, since the risk of bacteria and parasites can be extremely dangerous to pets whose immune systems are compromised.

Finally, if you have an FIV positive cat, it's important to get them **spayed or neutered.**

Bengal disorders

Your veterinarian is your partner in building the solid foundation of your cat's primary health care program. While any small animal veterinarian is qualified to work with your cat, I personally prefer my human to take my animals to a feline-specific clinic for a number of reasons.

- Feline-only vets stay on the cutting edge of medical development in the treatment of conditions exclusive to cats.

- The offices are much quieter. With no barking dogs or other unusual animals to startle your pets, the cats stay calmer and suffer less from anxiety. There are also fewer strange odours that put cats on high alert.

- Feline-only clinics understand "cat people" and our devotion to our animals. No one thinks anything about you admitting that you're a self-proclaimed "crazy cat lady," and you will never hear the abhorrent phrase, "just a cat."

In 2011, a scientific study revealed that Bengals are prone to **PRA** which is an **early onset primary photoreceptor disorder** – this leads to blindness within the first year of life in the cats that have it. Sadly, there isn't a test for it just yet, I'm sure there will be soon.

The study is actually online, it was written by a human called **Narfstrom et al -** you can just Google search the disorder and it comes up. I'll be honest, it was kind of a confusing read for me, because I'm a cat and it was clearly aimed at the science-community of humans. But it revealed some pretty important things about my breed.

Chronic Renal Failure can also be a tricky Bengal problem, although it's common in many breeds. Taking us to the vet for a check-up once a year so they can test for this is a fab idea. If your Bengal is particularly thirsty with a lack of interest in food or lethargy then it's worth taking the trip.

One of the biggest myths is that Bengal cats don't get **Feline Leukaemia Virus or FeLV**. I'm not sure where this even came from, but believe me we can catch the deadly FeLV just as easy as any other breed. FeLV is known as a retrovirus so as a consequence it will rewrite the RNA of a cell and then copy itself onto the DNA of other cells – WOW, pretty fascinating hey? Sadly, once this happens there is just no known way to halt it so this infectious disease will lead to untimely death.

If your human is choosing or interviewing a new vet, tell them to bring us along. Explain that you are coming to meet the doctor and to see the clinic and that you are perfectly happy to pay for a regular office visit.

Remember that veterinarians are medical professionals with a full roster of patients. Prepare your questions in advance and don't overstay. If you like what you see and hear, schedule a second visit that will include your family. The second visit is still for purposes of evaluation. You want to see how the vet and the techs interact with your pet.

- Are we reasonably relaxed in the office setting?
- Are we comfortable with the way we are being handled and treated?

Make sure that you are satisfied with the doctor, the staff, and the clinic before moving on to what will likely be your Bengals first official procedure, spaying or neutering.

CHAPTER EIGHT: Protect Your Bengal

I think I've made it perfectly clear throughout this book that Bengal's are extremely curious, sometimes to our own detriment. Being so inquisitive can sometimes get us into some nasty scrapes, but fortunately we have our loyal humans to look out for us!

So, here's how to take care of your Bengal and keep them safe...

Indoor vs. Outdoor

There is a lot of debate over whether or not cats should be allowed outside or kept indoors. But I'm here to tell you that both are totally acceptable lifestyles for your cat, I think it's both a personal and possibly cultural choice. It does however, depends on some important factors.

Outdoor:

Bengals are more active than most cats, and so being allowed outside helps us burn off some of our tenacity and most importantly, it keeps us from getting bored.

Getting bored is when most humans find we display behavioural problems, because we just have too much energy; our natural instinct is to run and hunt and have some space. I'm lucky, I live in an exceptionally quiet area, lots of great fields to explore nearby and no busy roads. Still – there's plenty of danger for me, I may get over excited and run too far, I could get chased by a grizzly dog, but as I said earlier, it's a personal cat and human choice. In my other house, I was near a main road, so my humans created an amazing outdoor space in the garden that I couldn't climb out of – clever things.

Before you let your Bengal cat outside, please, please, please make sure they are **micro-chipped** and identifiable just in case they get lost or hurt. But remember, don't let your Bengal outside until they're around 6 months old.

Bengals, in particular, are a lot more adventurous than other cats. We tend to roam further, so that our territory is larger. We also don't understand the concept of privacy. We're so fabulous, surely, we're welcome everywhere, so if we see an open door, we're probably going to go investigate and make ourselves at home. Depending on your neighbours and the door in question, there's a risk that we might get trapped or end up annoying people! (Who, me?)

Indoor:

One of the easiest advantages of keeping your cat indoors is that they'll may live longer. Cats that go outside are susceptible to road traffic accidents, getting into fights with other cats, and for us Bengals in particular, it's possible that we'll get stolen because we're valuable (and super good looking)!

If you're worried about the above issues, you can always let your cat outside under your supervision, or even try some harness training and get a lead for us to roam around on! Alternatively, you could do what Susan did at our ol d house and cat-proof your garden, or even build an outdoor enclosure!

As discussed previously, cats with FIV must be kept indoors to prevent risk of secondary infection and to reduce the chances of them passing on the disease.

At the end of the day, it really does depend on the area you live in, the personality of your cat, and how comfortable you feel with letting them outside. As long we have lots of love, lots of toys and stimulation then we are extremely happy inside.

Rehoming and shelters

As a rescue cat, of course I'm going to advocate that you adopt your cat rather than buy one from a breeder – but I would say that, wouldn't I? One potential problem with that is the personality traits or health background won't be known, so it really just depends how brave you are.

If you live in America, there are a couple of Bengal-specific rescue centres, such as Great Lakes Bengal Rescue and the Bengal Rescue Network (the latter extends to Canada, too). If you're reading all the way from Australia, there's an organisation called Bengal Rescue Australia that you can check out.

At home, here in the UK, you can look up specific breeders as they often have cats to rehome or you can find links via the Bengal Cat Club and have a good look on the Bengal Cat Forums too. There's a worldwide rehoming thread where people can put out ads for Bengals to be adopted to save them from having to go to a shelter. The cats are free to adopt (or require a small donation to a charity) and it's a great way of adopting a Bengal if you can't find a cat you love at your local shelter. Additionally, you can express your desire to adopt a cat on this thread and people looking to rehome their Bengals can contact you.

When you're at the shelter looking at all of the wonderful cats that need loving homes, here are some great tips to make sure you bring home the right cat for you.

Read their name plaques carefully.

As well as name and (predicted) age, these will often include some personality traits that the shelter workers have picked up on, and they aren't just throwing adjectives around! If a cat is described as 'playful' you can bet that they're going to be extra active, require frequent stimulation, and always be a playful cat. If a cat is described as being 'snuggly', then they're going to want lots of fuss and attention!

Has the cat been declawed? While a shelter should never declaw cats, it may be that they've rescued a cat that has already been declawed. This shouldn't put you off a cat, but it's important to consider so that you can be prepared for any potential nerve damage and the resulting physical limitations.

Good with other animals? You're adopting an animal that can live for almost two decades, so it's important to know whether the Bengal you're adopting is good with other animals. You may not have any other pets at the moment, but who knows what might happen 5, 10 or 15 years down the line!

At the end of the day, though, you'll just instinctively *know* when a cat is *your* cat. You'll feel it in the pit of your stomach and by the warmth in your heart when you meet them.

Choosing a Pedigree

If you've extensively searched your local shelters and still haven't found the Bengal for you, there is the option of buying your cat from a breeder. The cost of a Bengal should be between £500-1000 approximately (potentially slightly more or less) so be prepared to pay somewhere in that ball park. If you're looking to buy a show cat, then you're going to have to be willing to pay more money (£900+). If you're simply looking for a family pet, then you're likely to pay less money (£450-600) because breeders may have Bengals that are near perfect but not suitable for shows for whatever reason.

Buying a pedigreed Bengal can in no way be compared to simply picking out a kitten from a litter at a friend's house. In instances of unplanned litters, the human "parents" are generally all too ready to place us, the babies, in new homes and get the wandering mother cat "fixed" as soon as possible.

Pedigreed cats are not born by accident and they are not adopted out on a whim. It may come as something of a shock to you to learn that even if you are standing there cash in hand, you can be turned down by a breeder as a prospective Bengal Cat owner.

Under optimal circumstances you should find a breeder close to your area. Regardless, however, you should be prepared to go to the cattery in person and accompany your beautiful Bengal home either by car or plane. If you are flying with a kitten, pay to have the cat in the cabin with you, it's worth it, HONEST. No matter what guarantees are made for the safety and security of animals being shipped, the risks are far too great and the stresses too severe. In the vast majority of cases, breeders will not agree to ship kittens anyway, but I do not believe you should even consider this as an option.

Conditions of Purchase

You will usually be asked by the breeder to agree to some specific conditions in writing or you will certainly be denied the right to adopt a Bengal from the breeder in question.

Future Surrenders

For this reason, you will also be asked to agree that if you cannot keep your Bengal for any reason, you will never sell it to another person or give it to an animal shelter. If you must surrender the cat, you should contact the breeder. All breeders will take cats back rather than see them abandoned or placed in shelters only to be needlessly euthanized. The breeder's focus is rightfully on the welfare of the cat, and that extends to matters of re-homing should that become necessary.

Initial Health Evaluation

It's standard protocol to require a newly adopted pedigreed cat to be evaluated by a vet within 72 hours. You will be asked to provide written proof of this fact. The initial health evaluation is intended to provide a baseline for the health guarantee that is part of every adoption agreement. The vet visit confirms that when you received the kitten, the baby was in good health.

Lifestyle Inquiries

Although these questions are typically not asked in written format, the breeder will want to know about your home and your lifestyle. This isn't intended to be a matter of giving you the "third degree," so please don't be offended. Remember that breeders are passionately committed to the welfare of their cats; they want to know that we are going to good homes. Especially with a breed as interactive as a Bengal, the breeder will want to ascertain if have the time to give your new pet the attention and companionship it will crave.

In the weeks after the adoption, don't be surprised if the breeder calls you up to see how things are going. This isn't just checking up on the cat, but also to give you an opportunity to ask questions.

The owners of pedigreed cats should always be on friendly terms with the breeder from whom the animal was acquired. Your breeder is an expert on the Bengal breed an invaluable source of advice and information for you as you begin your life with your new baby.

Your Questions for the Breeder

Even though the breeder will want to get a lot of information from you, information should flow freely. You want to be dealing with someone who will freely answer your questions. Generally, this is not a problem. Breeders like nothing quite as much as talking about their cats.

Some of the questions you should ask include the following items, but don't limit yourself. The whole idea of this exchange is to ensure that both sides feel good about the adoption and about the living creature whose welfare and happiness should be central to the whole process.

- Are the kitten's parents healthy?
- What are their personalities like?
- Do they both live at the cattery?
- If not, where does the other parent reside?
- Can you see the health records for both parents?
- Can you meet and interact with the parents?
- Has the kitten received any vaccinations?
- Will those records be passed to you?
- Have other medical treatments been required?
- Has the kitten been dewormed?
- What health guarantees are included?
- Are references available?

In the matter of references, make sure you see not only written recommendations, but are also provided with the names and contact information of people willing to speak with you.

The Importance of Socialization

Typically, kittens remain in catteries until they are about three months old. By that time, they have been fully weaned and are reliably using both a litter box and a scratching post.

During the time the baby lives at the cattery, it should be exposed to various situations that help to achieve good socialization. As young cats, Bengals are highly adaptable, but as they age, they become used to their circumstances and less open to change.

Good socialization will help the kitten to have an easy transition to your home and to be better adjusted as an adult. Most Bengals (like me) will be somewhat shy around strangers, but you don't want your pet to be fearful of people who come into your home on a regular basis.

Organized socialization programs should include all of the following elements.

- **Daily handling.** Bengals are gregarious by nature and like to be a part of whatever is going on around them. They respond happily to being handled as kittens, although as adults they often prefer to initiate the interaction. This varies by individual.

- **Free exploration time.** This is also simply a matter of catering to the Bengals normally high level of curiosity. I wouldn't necessarily call the breed nosey but your cat will know every nook and cranny of your home, and few doors will be safe against those clever and dexterous paws.

- **Interaction with other cats.** Again, Bengal's are very social as kittens, so they should have lots of time to interact with other cats. If you're introducing a Bengal to a household with other pets, this is the ideal time to do it. As adults (like me) we can be territorial and occasionally a little jealous of our humans "special" people.

- **Access to plentiful toys.** Bengals are very playful. We love toys and are especially fond of long games of fetch. Find out what kind of toys the babies have liked at the cattery and get the same items for your home.

- **Exposure to normal household sounds.** Typically, Bengals are not nervous, but it is a good idea for us to be familiar with normal household sounds including appliances at a young age. All Bengals are prone to "thwacking" objects around the house, but this more an expression of playful dominance than fear.

Even for a gregarious breed like the Bengal, adoption still represents leaving the only environment they have known for a new home. Good socialization makes that change much easier.

Breeding Standards (UK / US)

UK Breeding Standards: If you're a reader from the UK, it's important you take a look at the Governing Council of the Cat Fancy (GCCF) organisation website, where you can check in with registered breed advisory committees and receive a list of reputable breeders in your area.

The GCCF has four key breeding rules that have to be followed:

1. Health must be the overriding consideration in any breeding programme.
2. The good (positive) and bad (negative) features of the individual cats should be assessed and weighed against each other before any mating. This includes the risk of passing on genetic faults/anomalies.
3. When planning a breeding programme, breeders must realise that doubling of the good traits in a cat may also result in doubling any defects; the breeding of cats with similar faults should be avoided at all costs otherwise there is a danger of fixation (i.e. creating a characteristic which cannot subsequently be eliminated).
4. Breeders must make themselves aware of the nature of the characteristics they wish to promote or avoid, whether these are due to a dominant gene (which will always be expressed when present) or a recessive gene (only expressed in the homozygous state i.e. where the cat inherits the gene from both parents).

They have a complete list of breeding policies on their website, which you can find here.

They also explain what you should look for in a Bengal, *"the Bengal should be alert, friendly and affectionate and in excellent physical condition with a dependable temperament. The Bengal's wild appearance is enhanced by its distinctive spotted or marbled tabby coat which should be thick and luxurious. The Bengal is a large to medium cat, sleek and muscular with a thick tail which is carried low. The females may be smaller than the males."*

They go into more detail in their short breed guide, which you can read in full here, which includes the Bengal breed point system.

US Breeding Standards: If you're an American reader, then The Cat Fancier's Association is the largest registry of pedigree cats, and should be your first port of call. They also have a Bengal breed guide and go into a similar point system as the GCCF. You can also find a kitten from a reputable breeder across the US by using their search feature.

Showing Cats

If you're interested in showing your cat, it's recommended that you first visit a show to see what's involved. It's important to consider whether or not **your cat will enjoy the experience**, shy or nervous cats will probably find shows stressful, and a show cat needs to be friendly and relaxed. This is especially important if your cat is non-pedigree, as these cats are mainly judged by their temperament.

It's best to introduce your cat to the show environment as a kitten so that they can get used to the environment early on.

You must also take into account the risk of infection. While every effort is made to ensure cats don't get sick, there is always the chance that your feline friend may become ill after a show, so you should weigh up whether that's a risk you're willing to take.

You should also think about whether your cat is "good enough" to be shown. Personally, I think every cat's a winner, but it's a good idea to ask a breeder or an experienced person who doesn't have rose-tinted goggles about your cat and see what they think!

The GCCF also list **pre-show preparation** and **show day information** on their website if you decide to go ahead with showing your cat!

Reputable vs. non-reputable breeders

In just a moment, I'm going to give you some easy pointers on how to tell if a breeder is reputable or not, but why is it important to buy from a reputable breeder?

Reputable breeders will care about the cats they produce. Parent cats are often their personal pets and the wellbeing of any kitten is important to them. Non-reputable breeders are only in this line of work to make a profit. They will often have a large number of animals in a small amount of space whose only purpose is to produce good looking kittens for them to sell on. Animals are often made to breed the moment they are able to, even though they are sometimes too small to withstand breeding comfortably.

When people continue to buy from non-reputable breeders, it keeps them in business and means that more animals will continue to be neglected or merely used for their reproductive abilities.

It's best to visit several breeders in your area to get a chance to compare. You'll be able to see the differences between several litters, and you'll feel less pressure to buy a kitten there and then because you've got options. A good breeder will be more than happy for you to go home and think about your decision before buying.

It's important to trust your gut when visiting breeders, if something doesn't feel right, then you have the ability to check out other breeders and see if your concerns were warranted. If breeders are unwilling to provide vaccination records, purchase contracts or pedigree records, then there are plenty more kittens in the sea!

What makes a breeder reputable?
If you live in America, the easiest way of telling if a breeder is reputable is if you live in a state that requires a cattery licence. That being said, a number of reputable breeders won't have licenses, most likely because they aren't required where they live.

There are lots of resources online giving recommended questions you should ask a breeder before you buy a kitten, so you should definitely have a pre-planned list of questions before you visit.

Here are some sure-fire ways of telling if you've found a good cat breeder:

- They encourage you to **visit them at their home**. Good cat breeders will always welcome future cat owners to come and visit them. This allows potential buyers to see how well the kittens are cared for, the environment they've been raised in and to see how healthy the other pets in the house are.
- Check the **kitten's health**. You can check the kitten's head, ears, eyes, nose, tummy and coat for anything that doesn't look right, and this will let you know if your kitten is healthy. If the kitten has a treatable illness like ear mites or fleas, these things are treatable but are also a testament to the responsibility of the breeder.
- They will be **passionate and knowledgeable** about the breed. A good breeder will be able to answer all your breed-specific questions and will be happy to describe the characteristics of their kittens for you. While good, passionate breeders will be knowledgeable, of course don't confuse shyness with being a bad breeder!
- They'll allow (and even encourage) you to **meet the kitten's parents**.
- They may **ask you lots of questions**, have you fill out a questionnaire, or even request a home visit. Don't be insulted by this, it means you're getting a kitten from a responsible breeder!

How to know if a breeder is non-reputable
Here are some red flags that should help you spot a bad breeder:

- Will appear nervous when answering questions about the breed, stammering, hesitating, etc.
- Will be unaware of the breed's genetic defects.
- Will have a lot of different breeds and too many cats in a small space with a few (if any) workers.
- Won't have much to say about their kitten's characters, instead focusing on titles.
- Only has bad things to say about other breeders.
- They don't ask you about you or the kind of home you'll be providing the kitten with.

- Will make excuses even when there's nothing to make an excuse about.
- They tell you that all cats of a specific breed have a specific problem, other than congenital defects, for example ear mites or ringworm.
- They are very insistent on you taking the kitten. They may lower the price, tell you that 'they'll go really fast so it's best to make a decision now' and so on.

Judging a Kitten's Health

Even though you have come to the breeder for the express purpose of adopting a kitten, always ask for permission to handle us. You may be asked to use hand sanitizer first. Don't be offended. This is for the protection of the kitten.

Beyond the fact that playing with an adorable baby kitten is a wonderful experience, it's also a great chance to evaluate our muscle tone as well as the quality and texture of our coat.

Bengal babies should have soft, clean coats that are completely intact with no thin spots. Check at the base of the tail, under the "arms" and behind the ears for any black gravel-like residue. This is known as "flea dirt" and is actually excreted bits of blood the parasites leave behind.

A kitten with one or two fleas is not being neglected or kept in poor conditions. The war on fleas is constant for all catteries, especially in warm weather. It's almost impossible not to bring the persistent pests in the house on your shoes or pants legs.

CHAPTER NINE: The Bengal Kitten

Here are some kitten-specific things you need to know before bringing your new Bengal kitty home.

Bringing your Bengal home

Bengals are the perfect family cats. As a breed, we are great with children because we love all the attention they give us! We're

also great cats to bring home if you also have a dog, because we're not scared of them. As long as they don't give your new kitten any problems, they might even become best friends, like me and Pepsi.

Other pets, even cats, in the house should be introduced slowly, and in a controlled environment. Let everyone get their bearings and they should all get along!

Like many cats, Bengals have a really high prey drive. Pets like hamsters, small rabbits or guinea pigs might not be safe around us, so either make sure we can't get to them, or consider waiting to get your Bengal until the smaller pets are no longer around.

While we do get on well with children, it is still important that you teach them the dos and don'ts of handling a cat. It's mostly common sense, but cats remember the things that scare them, and you wouldn't want your cat to be forever cautious around your children!

Within a few days of bringing your Bengal home, you should get them an appointment at the vets for a health check.

You should create a quiet space for your new kitten. Provide them with their own food and water bowl if you have other pets, and allow them to use this area as a retreat while they're settling in to your new home. After a week or so of settling in, slowly introduce your kitten to other rooms of the house and allow them to explore their new digs!

Kitten specific diet

It's best that you don't change your kitten's diet right away once you bring them home, so make sure you have plenty of the food they're used to before you pick them up. Sometimes people will give you a bag of food when you get your kitten, but if not it might be a good idea to take a picture of the food they eat so you can buy some yourself!

If you do want to change your kitten's diet, do it gradually as discussed in Chapter Four, but I strongly advise you hold off until your kitten has settled in to your home.

Toilet training

When you bring your kitten home, it is advised that you put a litterbox on every floor of your house. You should never rub your cat's nose in any accidents because we don't understand what that means. If you do catch us shortly after our accident, the best thing to do is remind us where our litterbox is.

Bengal kitten behaviour

I shouldn't have to say this, but it's important to never hit your cat. We're a lot less forgiving than dogs and it risks bringing out our defensive, aggressive side. If your Bengal exhibits displeasing behaviour, use a specific sound with your mouth or hands to tell us we're doing something wrong. In theory, the cat will then associate your action with bad behaviour and will learn when they are doing something that you don't like.

Some people suggest you get a spray bottle and squirt water at your cat when they misbehave, but given that we love water, that's not really a punishment for Bengals!

The best way to train your kitten is through positive reinforcement, remember I told you about clicker training? The younger you start teaching us, the quicker we'll catch on!

If your kitten is rough housing with you and starts biting or scratching you, remain still, as though playing dead, and distract them with a toy with your other hand. If you try and pull your hand away, they'll think it's part of the game and get more excited. You don't want any nasty bites! Likewise, if your cat gets their paws on something you don't want them playing with, engage with them using a different toy and then hide the original item while they're distracted.

It is never a good idea to play with your cat using just your hands. You don't want them to associate your hands as toys, so to teach your cat that aggression towards hands isn't acceptable, always play with a toy!

Kittens usually have a mad 20-30 minutes of hard play in the evenings before they tucker themselves out and go to sleep. I still do it though, not sure why I haven't quite grown out of it yet. Susan's fault not mine, hee hee.

Teething

Kittens start to lose their milk teeth (baby teeth) when they're around eleven weeks old. At four months old, all of their permanent incisors should have come through, and by five months they'll have all their canines.

During the teething period, your kitten will have sore gums and so they may be a little rougher while playing, appear agitated, and start chewing things to seek relief.

My friend Levy chewed the carpets, chair legs, bottoms of the doors, fingers, feet and just about anything hard while he was teething. His owner used a sneaky trick, and put some of his cat meat gravy on a hide chew to distract him from chewing the wrong things!

While your kitten is teething, you shouldn't encourage their rough playing; they might catch or scrape their gums so it's best to keep rough play to a minimum. You should also avoid brushing your kitten's teeth during this period. It will cause more pain and will cause them to associate brushing their teeth with pain and discomfort.

Also, avoid feeding your kitten hard food that requires a lot of chewing during this period. If your kitten *enjoys* chewing, try mixing their wet food with dry during their teething months.

Most kittens end up eating or swallowing their baby teeth, which is normal and nothing to worry about. You also shouldn't be alarmed if you find some milk teeth around the house after they've fallen out!

Signs something might be wrong:

-   Excessive meowing might indicate your kitten is in pain because of unusual teething problems, which may be cause for concern.

-   Changes in eating habits, such as avoiding dry food, would suggest your kitten might prefer wet food during this period. But if they stop eating altogether, you should see your vet ASAP.
-   Finding a little blood on your kitten's toys or things they've chewed is not uncommon, but if your kitten's mouth is bleeding regularly or you notice a significant amount of blood you should see your vet ASAP.

- If you notice a lot of swelling around your kitten's mouth, see your vet ASAP.

How to help your teething kitten:

- Cover all your wires. They're often the main victim of a teething kitten so it's best to keep all your wiring covered up and as unappealing to your kitten as possible.

- You can buy kitten teething toys, made of high quality material designed to last.

- Cat grass is a great source of relief through chewing. Its soft and cool texture is great for soothing sore kitty gums, as well as being good for the immune system, and preventing hairballs! You can even grow you own!

The Elderly Bengal

A lot of cats will start showing physical signs of aging once they reach around 7-12 years old. As cats get older, this might mean they lose their appetite, have less energy or difficulty walking.

So, to prepare you for your Bengal's golden years, here are some tips on how to help your cat age gracefully!

Elderly Bengals at home

While you probably won't need to adapt your home in any major capacity as your Bengal gets older, there are some subtle changes you can make to help ease them into the transition of senior cat life.

If you've gone to the shelter and adopted an older cat, you should be prepared for them to exhibit behaviours that could well be lifelong habits. If your adopted Bengal displays undesirable behaviours then use the suggestions in previous chapters to train them, just bare in mind that with adopted older cats, it may take them longer to break their habits.

It's a good idea to invest in an extra litterbox. Much like when you're first toilet training a kitten, you may want to have a litterbox on every floor of your home for your elderly Bengal.

Another thing that humans like to do is get raised platforms for food and water bowls, so that their older cats don't have to bend down as much to eat and drink – humans are so thoughtful! Speaking of food…

Changes in diet

As cats get older, there's a bigger risk of a large number of diseases. Obesity can also contribute to this susceptibility, especially to diabetes and skin problems. Older cats can lose weight and muscle, so it's important to adjust your cat's diet from age 10.

Regardless of whether your cat is showing physical signs of aging, you should start adjusting your cat's diet at age 10 in order to address any metabolic changes.

You can find lots of cat foods online or at your local shop for elder cats, but as always, I recommend you consult your vet before changing your cat's diet.

Index

S

Salmonella, 30
Scent Marking, 23
scratching, 39
scratching posts, 40
Seal lynx point, 10
Seal mink, 10
Seal sepia, 11
second cat, 19
Sheeted / closed pattern, 12
shout, 24
showing, 56
Silver, 10
silver rosettes, 11
Single-spotting, 14
sleep, 41
Snow, 10
snow marble, 11
solitary, 7
spots, 13
Spraying, 21
stability, 25
Stress, 21
stripes, 9

T

Tapeworms, 44
Temperament, 20
territorial, 19
The International Cat Association, 7
tomatoes, 31

toys, 35
translucent hair shafts, 15
tricks, 16
Tri-colour, 12
Trim, 40

U

UK Breeding Standards, 55
Urine Off, 24
US Breeding Standards, 56

V

Vaccines, 42
vitamins, 29
vocal, 17

W

water, 28
William Centerwall, 7
Worming, 44
worms, 27

X

Xylitol, 31

Y

Yeast dough, 32

Z

Zylkene, 22

Made in the USA
Coppell, TX
22 August 2020

33978353R40066